A Darkness of Mooses

AF624548

Rachel de Moose

BookLeaf Publishing

Presentation by *BookLeaf Publishing*

Web: www.bookleafpub.com

E-mail: info@bookleafpub.com

ISBN: 9789357211222

First edition 2022

DEDICATION

For Toni, who departed this spinning rock far too young. She still invades all my music playlists, and I wouldn't have it any other way. I miss her every single day.

ACKNOWLEDGEMENT

I owe my passion for poetry to two people: my mother, Denise E. Salembier, and my dearly departed grandmother, Marilyn H. Salembier.

My mom is the best person to grace this Earth, and she fostered a creative environment for me from a very early age. We read anything from Dr. Seuss to Emily Dickinson. As I discovered more and more literary works, I stumbled upon Edgar Allan Poe and immediately fell in love. In school, we read "Annabel Lee" and it hooked me immediately. Right then and there, I decided that was my favorite poem. I learned from my mom, that same day, that "The Bells" was her favorite poem...also by Edgar Allan Poe.

I grew up far away from my grandma, who lived in Southwest Florida. However, we chatted on the phone often, frequently for hours at a time. I always knew she was a music minor; however, in college I learned she majored in English, exactly like me. She wrote her own works frequently, and she preferred poetry, also exactly like me. She sent me one of her poems, about Autumn, that she never shared with anyone before. I felt so special, and I've always treasured these similarities within us.

PREFACE

tl;dr: Here is my soul in written form. Most of these poems have never seen the light of day by anyone but myself. Enjoy the stream of consciousness from the depths of my mind.

Caught in a Memory

I always wanted to be like Sailor Moon,
no- Sailor Jupiter. Sailor Moon was too whiny.
Whenever I needed courage, I would close my
eyes
and think about the Scouts saving the world.

I played kickball better than half the boys,
and tore through arms made of Red Rover steel.

My friend taught me to ride a bike
after my precious Bigwheel saw its last day.
Elton John music filled the bedroom, as usual.

I spent half my days climbing trees
and exploring on the bike I was so proud to ride.

I used to stealthily slip out my door at 3am,
just so I could visit the park and climb my
favorite tree.
My tree brought joy, peace, and clarity.
I was on top of the world- unstoppable,
invincible.

My favorite person in the world
should have taught me those activities
and shared those wonderful memories with me.

She would chase my monsters away from the
dark
with her sweet melodies and a kiss good night.

Unsung Lullaby

You were only around a little while, but I
ballooned like a party favor anyway.
We laughed when I had to buy new
clothes,
and don sweatshirts- even when
it was too warm.

I enjoyed talking to you, wondering if you
could hear me. But I didn't care.
I kept talking for hours anyway.
Many nights I even sang you to sleep- as
if you were the one who needed sleep.

I was very protective of you, right from the
very beginning.
Your discontent became my own, as my wish
was for you to always be happy.
I used to rub my belly often to make you
feel better.

I dreamed often about what you would be like
when you got here.
Anytime I was in a clothing store, I
unconsciously drifted to your section.
I always loved those little tiny shoes.

You were only around a little while,
but that's all it took.
My love began instantaneously, as if there were
no other choice in the world.

Mister Sinister

You say you're sorry, but you get into trouble
anyway.
Your thoughts are like scrabble pieces,
struggling to come together and make sense.
If only someone could give you a clue,
some catch phrase to slide you by.
Your memory struggles to reject the taboo ideas.
You long to set up a mouse trap for them
and feel the joy of them going splat!
Keep it all in. Don't spill the beans.
Your brain secretly enjoys the trivial pursuit.
Picking it apart feels like an operation.

Neverland

dress, billowing in the wind
I twirl around in the illuminated darkness.
pretty stars that go
twinkle twinkle catch my eye
11:11 must make a wish.

it would be amazing to be on an island
and sleep in hammocks. you
know, like Gilligan did.
give me a pineapple smoothie
and my day's complete
why does it have to be so
cold?
work sucks where's my island
when I need it?
I want my pineapple smoothie under
the stars!
when I was little, I wanted to ride in a
kangaroo's pouch
it would be like snuggling in a heated stroller,
but much comfier.
you get to bounce around everywhere!
I want to fly like Peter
to my island.

my version

of

[Neverland]

Sunshine and rain

I feel the warmth wrap me in its blanket.

The light breeze tousles my hair, revealing its
bounce.

Light is shed on my smile.

The world has been illuminated by the
biggest star in the universe.

The rain rolls in.

Thunder booms. Lightning strikes.

I feel an eerie sense of peace.
The roaring thunder makes me giggle.

I twirl in circles.

People across the way run for cover, afraid.
I let the downpour embrace me.

Drenched and unabashed, I go for a stroll in the park, hand-in-hand

With my best friends   sunshine and rain.

Epiphany

you crossed my mind, leaving me unaffected.
all I felt was pure shock.
there's a first time for everything, I suppose.
warm weather's been known to do wonders for my mood.
the whole 'crying over you' charade is getting old.
I've pictured in my head countless times the scene where you sweep me off my feet
and whisper how much you've missed me,
you can't live without me.
you need me forever, you've always felt it.
my feet are planted on reality ground,
accepting what won't happen.
I've fought to silence the girl who wants more for herself.
someone who listens is endearing,
something I need to remember.
looks like I'm not afraid of being over you-
I'm afraid of what happens after.
the afterlife is always intimidating.

I'll be okay, don't you worry.
not that you would anyway.

Life=Broad

I don't like nights when it's too cloudy to see the stars.

Stars are peaceful. Lying upon my car, gazing upward, connecting the dots.

There's a certain comfort in the night,
Hidden by rapists and creepy animals.

Death itself isn't the scary part. The fear is in what, if anything, comes after.
It's another journey into a new world.

Death is the downside of life.
Miracle children are born, the wise pass on.

Some can't wait to be awake to fill the days with all the clichés I could use.
The mornings you wish to stay in bed all day.

Does the rainbow know it's beautiful?
All the colors are there for people to fawn over.

Thunder claps against your head.
Lightning bolts all around.
The day where nothing goes right.

Warm days on the beach when the sunlight
shines over the ocean, making it sparkle.
You close your eyes, drinking it all in.

I'll Be Seeing You

You couldn't have known your fate,
for I didn't either.
I used to giggle as my belly got bigger,
wondering when my feet would turn into a magician
and wow me with their disappearing act.
Night after night I dreamed of snuggling you to my bosom
and lullabying you to sleep.
Touch those plump, soft cheeks
and watch you smile amidst your slumber.
Seeing you so peaceful would lull me to sleep as well.
While you were around, I would play Elton John music for you
as my mother did for me.
I think you liked it, because my stomach wasn't upset on those days.
Eventually, those days will start again,
and I'll always wonder about you and how you would have turned out,
if Fate hadn't stolen you away.
I know I'll be seeing you one day in a new place
and know you were mine,

even if only for a little while.

Mr. Big

I started my car, wiping my tears
as all his other girlfriends stared
everyone was laughing
I said to him as I glared,
"how many? one, two… how long?"
it's a strange thought,
to know I'm not the only one.
seconds passed with no answer,
as everyone whispered intently,
taking bets on the heart-wrenching outcome.
he sauntered away, hand-in-hand with some
tramp.
my tears ran dry at this point.
I figured I never meant enough anyway.
I'm going home through the front door for once.
confused.

Whimsy

as whale-shaped clouds trail by
I sit with my dinosaur chicken nuggets
and strawberry Ariel fruit snacks.
in my eyes, I'm a sea princess.
I'm all bedazzled in my dress-up tutu
paired over my flared jeans and black polo.
my boyfriend comes over-
we roll down hills and blow dandelions.
nothing else matters but that moment
where we lay laughing 'til we cry.
we hop into my car
and drive to FunTime America to play laser-tag
with me still wearing the tutu.
except now I'm carrying a magic wand.
I can grant wishes!
when we pull into the parking lot
I open the glove compartment and pull out
a container of Mott's applesauce and a spoon.
I can balance spoons on my nose!
we run around with the 10-year-olds,
with me still in my pretty pink glittery tutu.
people gawk at us 20-year-olds
as if we had a serious mental problem.
click your heels three times and you'll be in
Neverland.

do you think I can fly?

Truth or Dare

truth or dare.
red rover.   ring around the rosy.
      kickball.   jump rope.

games of   childhood.

red rover, red rover, I call gener over!

        99 monkeys, jumping on the bed!
one fell off and bumped its head!

        whimsical spinning in the grass.   juice
boxes.
              my bigwheel will take me anywhere.

hakuna matata! it means no worries

              hopscotch. around the world.

        manhunt. ollie-ollie-oxen-free!

when you're a child you long to be grown up.
                  when you're grown up you long to
be a child.

childhood always seems so innocent and
carefree,
free of emotional
spiderwebs.

the problem is,
the spiderwebs are made of steel,
and no matter how hard you
fight to tear it down
it's always there, glaring at you with
spite.

truth or dare. i dare you to love me.
ashes, ashes, we all fall down.

Hello

Hey you, out there alone
what are you doing?
Skipping stones and dancing oddly…
are you doing the Crocodile Rock?
I like Elton John, he's my favorite.
Why are you hunched over like that?
You don't look very happy.
could you turn so I can see your face?
Oh my….it's you.
I didn't realize that, though I should've.
It's been a long time since I've seen you.
I've replayed in my head what I'd say,
you know, if I ever saw you again.
of course, now I can't remember a damn word.
It's those eyes of yours…every time I look,
no, gaze- I stumble over myself.
I really never thought I'd see you again.
It's kind of awkward,
but thrilling at the same time.
My heart's pounding so hard and skipping beats.
is that normal?
Oh, yeah, I forgot- you do that to me every time
I see you.
The only problem is, my heart has now
plummeted to my stomach

and it's thrashing about in pain.
And here I was thinking I was healed.
You've always enjoyed proving me wrong.
Why do you look at me with such disdain,
as if I was the one who caused all the turmoil?
No, don't even try to apologize.
It'll hurt too much,
and I'll fall apart again when I was so convinced
I was sewn back together.
No, you don't have to leave. I will.
maybe I'll see you around again sometime.
Oh, by the way-
hello. I love you.

Under Lock and Key

These thoughts swirling in my head have me in a bind…
What do I do?
I really like him,
But I still love someone else-
-no, must push that out.
I'm not allowed to think that.
I'm not allowed to listen to songs that remind me of him,
Or look at our old pictures.
No, it's wrong. Forget it.
But I really like this new guy…
Rough around the edges but sweet,
Ever so sweet…
Reminds me a lot of- no, stop!
He'd hate that. They hate each other.
I'll never have him again, so push it out.
I'm history to him- we're just a faded memory.
Gotta focus on what I've got,
Not what I'll never have again.
His girl is the luckiest one alive.
He's gone… and I feel empty.
No, gotta block that out.
Maybe I've got enough love for this guy?
Do I even have anything left?

Or does the other still have my heart?
Questions best left unanswered…

Passion, Remorse, Hatred, and Bliss

I see you glance at me from across the room,
With those daring lips of yours.
Lips I want to kiss,
Feel the passion in your hips,
And experience true bliss.
In your mind you feel the empty void in your heart,
Aching from having lost someone,
Remorse for letting them go.
You look for someone to fill that void,
And when you see her your heart races.
Those curves, the way she glances back at you, she has no idea you won't be around tomorrow or next week.
You stifle the hatred you feel for yourself, shove it aside,
Lock it deep inside a crevasse and throw away the key,
Because in this moment, right now, she just looks too insatiable to resist.

Comfortable Lie

Deep down, I knew nothing would happen.
You were such a sweet-talker,
it wasn't long before I believed anything you said to me.
It seemed like such a sure thing.
We seemed like such a sure thing.
Where we were was so comfortable;
your words were like satin sheets,
soothing me with every syllable.
I was so content to play along,
as long as there was a possibility of having you in the end.
I really thought there was,
but what a big lie that turned out to be...
...just like everything else you said to me.
All of our conversations...
our telephone calls...
the late night text messages...
the thoughts you'd engrave in my head...
you were such a sweet-talker.
What a comfortable lie.

Letter to a Future Grandchild

My Dear Granddaughter,

I love you and I miss you! I hope everything at home is good and I am thrilled for the next time I see you.

I know you are moving into a new phase of your life and wanted to impart a little wisdom I feel I learned too late. Do not let fear hold you back from doing what you want. If you love someone, tell them. If you grow tired of your career, find a new one. Continue your education if you feel you have more to learn. Travel if you want to explore the world.

We all have fears, and they are crippling. They freeze you in time, immobilize you, and manipulate you into inaction. Wayne Gretzky said it best: "You miss 100% of the shots you don't take." Take the shot. Even if you miss, you can still end up somewhere great, and you will have other chances.

Love,
Grandma

Stepping Stones, Desires

Stepping Stones

I was born
I began to walk
I began school
I was classified as Developmentally Delayed
I began speech therapy
I was de-classified after 4th grade
I had my first boyfriend
I met my best friend
I was sexually assaulted
I earned my driver's license
I graduated high school
I began college, then left for financial reasons
I was asked to leave my father's house
I moved in with my mom
I began dating my current boyfriend
I lost my best friend due to a car accident
I had three miscarriages
I was in a debilitating car accident
I received my Associate's Degree
I recovered from my accident

Desires

I wanted to go to school
I wanted to feel normal
I wanted to live with my mom again
I wanted to grow taller
I wanted to join the school band
I wanted to die
I wanted to live
I wanted to learn French
I wanted to kiss boys
I wanted to kiss girls
I wanted to be a Special Education teacher
I then wanted to be a counselor
I wanted a healthy relationship
I wanted financial stability
I wanted a college degree
I wanted my best friend back
I wanted to get pregnant again
I wanted to be a Clinical Psychologist

Blended Desires
I wanted to go to school
I began school
I was classified as Developmentally Delayed
I began speech therapy
I wanted to feel normal
I was de-classified after 4th grade
I had my first boyfriend
I was sexually assaulted
I wanted to die

I met my best friend
I wanted to live
I began college, then left for financial reasons
I wanted to be a Special Education teacher
I then wanted to be a counselor
I wanted a college degree
I got my Associate's Degree
I wanted to be a Clinical Psychologist
I wanted a healthy relationship
I began dating my current boyfriend
I had three miscarriages
I wanted to get pregnant again
I lost my best friend due to a car accident
I wanted my best friend back

Fairytale

Once upon a time, there was a woman who deeply adored a man. This man was kind, caring, funny, and intelligent. He was well-educated and loved his family. They had been friends for 14 years, and were only a few months apart in age. He had a responsible work ethic and was diligent in his duties. However, he lived in their hometown in New Jersey, and she had moved out of state to Pennsylvania three years prior.

Since she moved, her contact with this man was brief and fleeting. He worked long, arduous hours, and he was so exhausted that her messages were often unreturned. Finally, after those three long years, she managed to arrange to have dinner with him one night. She was dumbfounded by how easy it was to pick up where they left off last time they saw each other. It was effortless, and the more they ate, the more she realized how much she adored him and longed to be with him. After those few hours, though, the evening was over and she drove back the next day to Pennsylvania.

Over the next 4 months, she could not shake him from her mind. He popped in constantly, and she found herself daydreaming at work about him. She fought to keep him out of her mind because of the distance, and because she feared he would not return her sentiments. After these 4 months of wrestling with herself, she mustered up the courage to ask him on a date. She was sick and tired of sitting idly by while her chances at happiness slipped away. She wanted to embrace happiness, rather than shrivel back from it in fear. Much to her surprise and excitement, he accepted. They began their journey together on that first date and have been together ever since.

Memories of My Mom

What memories do I have of my mom?

I remember her pulling me out of the swimming pool when I was drowning at the age of three.

I dove in with nobody unaware so she frantically jumped in.

I remember her losing her hair from her cancer treatment. I was only 6 and didn't understand anything about cancer. I didn't even know that's what she had. I just knew she was really sick and I wanted to do everything I could to make her feel better.

I remember the paralysis that came from her chemotherapy.

I remember crying five years later when she took her first steps without her cane in the house, unsupported.

I remember the day I was taken away from her.

I remember crying at the fence at school, barred from going home with her.

I remember the nine years after that I couldn't spend a night with her.

I remember driving to her house and spending my first night with her since, at the age of 18, after telling my father I was at my best friend's house.

I remember moving back in with her at 23.

I remember finding out she and her now wife were finally getting married, after over 20 years of being together.

I remember the song they danced to at the reception.

I still get teary when I tell people they danced to "At Last" by Etta James.

I remember the day these burdens finally fell off my shoulders.

Riptides

The water was choppy,
undertow so forceful it knocked you on your knees.
The slant of the tide eerily indicated riptides.
I gazed up in awe at the towering swells,
longing to be in that water.
A rush coursed through my veins every time I leapt over giant waves,
and I yearned to tackle these Hawaii-esque swells.
I argued with myself for an hour, nervous;
the waves crashed back-to-back with a thundering force.
I finally spotted an opening and seized my only chance.
Despite knowing better, I sloshed in.
I dove under a massive curl, milliseconds too soon.
I spun around like a cyclone for what felt like an eternity,
barely breaking the surface before being dragged under again.
The tide forced my body into somersaults,
grinding my face into the sand repeatedly,
beating me into a pulp.

I gasped for air,
waving frantically for help anytime I surfaced.
I felt myself beginning to black out.
Finally, a momentary lull sent me to the surface,
washing ashore with water in my lungs.
With jelly legs, I collapsed, unable to walk or
move.
I was beached.

Toni

I mourn two days every year.
March 31st, 2014: the day my best friend
sustained life threatening injuries from a
debilitating car accident.
April 3rd, 2014: the day she died, after being
declared legally brain dead.
I can't bear to hear people joke about being
"brain dead" anymore if they forget something.
I cherish letters and photos more than ever.
I see signs everywhere.
She invades my music playlists.
I fundamentally changed as a person.
She took part of my heart with her when she left.
(Cliché, I know. I don't care.)
I saved all our online conversations and read
through them occasionally.
I think about traditional words of comfort when
someone dies.
They do nothing for me.
Don't tell me she's in a better place.
Don't tell me God called her home.
Don't tell me it will be okay.
I am okay, as a person, 8 years later.
NOTHING will ever make losing her okay.

I hair pull. I fight the urge to self-harm, and I succeed.
You may think me weak;
I think I'm strong beyond measure.
More than anything, I remember good times.
I remember when we met.
I remember picking out clothes for her.
I remember her overtaking my playlists in the car.
I remember her napping everywhere.
I remember her eating everything off the Taco Bell menu.
I remember her loving shopping but hating rifling through racks of clothes.
I remember her loving the beach but rarely venturing into the water.
I remember her taking blurry selfies of everything and everyone.
I remember never being able to understand her on the phone.
Above all, I remember.
It's all I have left.

www.ingramcontent.com/pod-product-compliance
Lightning Source LLC
Chambersburg PA
CBHW051741130826
49812CB00033B/958
* 9 7 8 9 3 5 7 2 1 1 2 2 2 *